Screws in Action

Gillian Gosman

PowerKiDS
press.

New York

Published in 2011 by The Rosen Publishing Group, Inc.
29 East 21st Street, New York, NY 10010

First Edition

Editor: Maggie Murphy
Book Design: Kate Laczynski
Photo Researcher: Jessica Gerweck

Photo Credits: Cover, pp. 4, 5, 6, 7 (top), 10, 11 (top), 18, 19, 22 Shutterstock.com; p. 7 (bottom) Cavan Images/Getty Images; p. 9 Kevin Cooley/Getty Images; p. 11 (bottom) © www.iStockphoto.com/David Freund; pp. 12, 16 SSPL/Getty Images; p. 13 Roger Viollet/Getty Images; p. 14 Three Lions/Getty Images; p. 15 Popperfoto/Getty Images; p. 17 © www.iStockphoto.com/Steve Shepard; pp. 20, 21 © Rosen Publishing.

Library of Congress Cataloging-in-Publication Data

Gosman, Gillian.
  Screws in action / Gillian Gosman. — 1st ed.
      p. cm. — (Simple machines at work)
  Includes index.
  ISBN 978-1-4488-0686-7 (library binding) — ISBN 978-1-4488-1305-6 (pbk.) — ISBN 978-1-4488-1306-3 (6-pack)
  1. Screws—Juvenile literature. I. Title.
  TJ1338.G67 2011
  621.8'82—dc22

                                                    2010003768

Manufactured in the United States of America

CPSIA Compliance Information: Batch #WS10PK: For Further Information contact Rosen Publishing, New York, New York at 1-800-237-9932

What Is a Screw?

A power drill, such as this one, can apply the force needed to twist a screw into a wall.

In its most common form, a screw is a tool that holds things in place. When you apply **force** to the top of a simple wood screw by turning it with a drill or screwdriver, the screw twists directly into another **material**, often wood or plaster. Other screws are used to lift things or to put **pressure** on another object, as is the case with a vise, a **clamp**, or a monkey wrench.

A screw is one of six simple machines. The other machines are the wedge, the **inclined plane**, the wheel and axle, the pulley, and the lever. All of these simple machines have few or no moving parts. They can be put together in different ways to make **compound** machines.

Many wrenches have a screw that lets you move the part of the wrench that holds another object. This way it can hold objects of many sizes.

5

The Parts of a Screw

This picture shows many kinds of screws, bolts, and nuts.

A wood screw is a short metal bar in the shape of a **cylinder**. At one end of the cylinder, there is a flat or rounded head with a slot into which a screwdriver's tip fits. At the other end, the cylinder comes to a point. Along the shaft, or length, of the screw is a metal ridge wound in a **spiral** shape.

Here you can see the thread of a screw. This metal ridge wraps in a spiral around the screw's cylindrical base.

This spiral ridge is called the screw's thread.

A screw can also take other forms, such as a ceiling fan, a corkscrew, or an airplane **propeller**. Each of these tools or machines has different special parts, but they all work like a simple wood screw.

An airplane propeller may not look like a screw. However, it twists in a circle and cuts through the air as a screw cuts through wood or plaster.

What Makes a Screw Special?

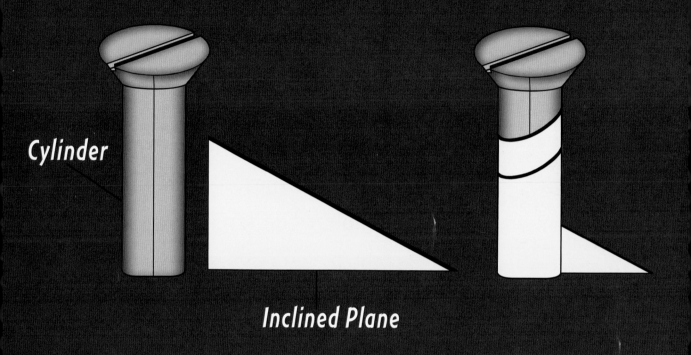

Cylinder

Inclined Plane

The thread of a screw is really an inclined plane wrapped around a cylinder. As rotational, or turning, force is applied to the top of a wood screw, the plane of the thread meets and lifts the material around it. The **mechanical advantage** of a screw depends on how thick the cylinder is. It also depends

8

This picture shows how a screw's thread is the same as an inclined plane's slope. The slope of the inclined plane is the black edge of the triangle.

on how close together the ridges of the threads are. The closer together the threads are, the greater the mechanical advantage of the screw.

Screws are often used to hold things in place. They do this much better than nails because the threads cut into the material and hold the screw in place.

Here, a woman twists a screw into a wall with a screwdriver.

The Screw at Work

There are different kinds of screwdrivers made for different kinds of screws.

A wood screw is driven into and pulled out of a material with the help of a drill or screwdriver. The tip of the drill or screwdriver is placed in the slot at the top of the screw and twists the head of the screw. The threads of the screw then cut into the wood, holding the screw in place or working to pull the screw in or out.

The spiral ridge on the inside of this bottle cap is an interlocking thread.

A screw's thread may also meet an **interlocking** thread in the material around it. For example, the thread on the inside of a bottle cap is meant to interlock with the thread around the mouth of the bottle. However, if the two threads do not meet the right way, the screw will jam, or stop.

The interlocking thread on the mouth of this bottle keeps the cap from falling off.

An ancient Greek mathematician named Archimedes is believed to be the **inventor** of the screw pump, the first machine that used the idea of the screw. The screw pump is also called

12

Archimedes' screw. Archimedes invented this machine in the third century BCE.

The screw pump is used to lift water from low-lying ground to higher ground. It is a large metal screw inside a metal pipe. A windmill or handle at the top of the pipe turns the screw. As the screw turns, water is lifted up and out of the top of the pipe. This water is often used to water crops.

A drawing of the inventor Archimedes is shown here. Archimedes also invented machines that made use of other simple machines, such as the lever.

13

Screws Through Time

This drawing shows a large screw press used for making coins in the Middle Ages.

Since Archimedes' time, screws have come in every size and material. Wagon wheel screws were made of wood. Tiny screws made of brass and other metals were used in watches, scientific tools, and jewelry.

Throughout history, people have used the power of the screw to do many different jobs. Around the year

1440, German craftsman Johannes Gutenberg used the idea of the fruit press to build the first screw press for printing books. In the late 1500s, inventors used Gutenberg's ideas to create a screw press for making coins.

Here, you can see a drawing of Johannes Gutenberg's first printing press.

15

Screws on the Job

The steam hammer, shown here, was a tool used for shaping pieces of metal in the mid-1800s. You can see large screws, which allowed people to move the machine's parts, in this steam hammer.

Throughout history, the screw press has done many jobs in factories. Some screw presses are used in forging, which is the shaping of metal by applying pressure. These screw presses can bend, cut, stamp, or flatten sheets and pieces of metal.

Other screw presses are used to compact, or press together, materials. Today, many of these machines are powered by engines or computers. However, in the past, they were built on the idea of the simple screw. Like Gutenberg's early printing press, the factory screw press uses the power of the screw to apply different amounts of pressure as needed.

A pipe clamp, such as this one, is another kind of machine that uses a screw to press materials together or hold them in place. Pipe clamps are often used in woodworking shops.

Screws All Around

Here you can see a nut (left) and a bolt (right). There is a thread on the inside of the nut that interlocks with the thread of the bolt.

Most of the screws you see around your classroom and home are holdings things together or in place. The chairs you sit on, the **hinges** on doors, and the lightbulbs in lamps are all held together or in place by the power of the screw.

Another screw you might see often is called a bolt. A bolt is a special kind of screw used to hold things together. It has a flat end and a matching nut, or a ring of metal with interlocking threads. You are using the idea of the bolt and nut when you twist a lid onto a screw-top jar or screw in a lightbulb.

The thread on the bottom of a lightbulb, shown here, interlocks with the thread in the lightbulb socket on a lamp.

An Experiment with a Screw

A screw is an inclined plane wrapped around a cylinder. You can move a load quickly up a short, steep inclined plane, but it will be difficult. It is easier to push or pull a load up a longer, less steep incline, but it will take more time. A screw with few threads per inch (cm) is like a short, steep inclined plane. A screw with more threads per inch (cm) is like a longer, less steep inclined plane. A simple **experiment** will prove this.

What You Will Need:
- a hammer
- a nail
- a piece of wood
- a screwdriver
- two screws of about the same length, one with twice as many threads per inch (cm) than the other has
- an adult to help you

step 2

1. Have an adult hammer a nail slightly into a piece of wood. This will make a small hole in which the tip of a screw can fit.

2. Take the screw that has fewer threads and screw it into the starter hole. How difficult is it to screw it into

the wood? How many turns of the screwdriver does it take to twist it into place?

3. Have the adult make a second starter hole.

4. Twist the screw that has more threads into place. Is it easier to twist this screw into the piece of wood? Does it take more twists of the screwdriver?

step 4

The Super Strength of Screws

Screws are also used to lift heavy loads. Two of the most common screw jacks, or lifting machines, are the car jack and the house jack.

A car jack is a machine that allows a person to slowly raise a car, in order to make repairs or replace

a flat tire. House jacks allow workers to raise a whole house above its foundation, or base. This is often done so that workers can rebuild or strengthen the foundation. Screws are very strong!

Glossary

clamp (KLAMP) A tool that holds things tightly together.

compound (KOM-pownd) Two or more things put together.

cylinder (SIH-len-der) A tubelike object.

experiment (ik-SPER-uh-ment) A set of actions or steps taken to learn more about something.

force (FORS) Something that moves or pushes on something else.

hinges (HINJ-ez) Bendable parts.

inclined plane (in-KLYND PLAYN) A simple machine with a sloped surface.

interlocking (in-ter-LOK-ing) Connecting together.

inventor (in-VEN-tur) Someone who designs or creates something new.

material (muh-TEER-ee-ul) What something is made of.

mechanical advantage (mih-KA-nih-kul ud-VAN-tij) The help a machine gives.

pressure (PREH-shur) A force that pushes on something.

propeller (pruh-PEL-er) Paddlelike parts on an object that spin to move the object forward.

spiral (SPY-rul) Curved or curled.

Index

Web Sites

Due to the changing nature of Internet links, PowerKids Press has developed an online list of Web sites related to the subject of this book. This site is updated regularly. Please use this link to access the list:

www.powerkidslinks.com/sm/screw/

24